Stars of Mythology

CHINESE

Nancy Dickmann

W
FRANKLIN WATTS
LONDON • SYDNEY

Franklin Watts

First published in Great Britain in 2017
by The Watts Publishing Group

Credits
Series editor: Sarah Peutrill
Series design and illustrations: Matt Lilly
Cover design: Cathryn Gilbert
Picture researcher: Diana Morris

Pic credits: Bigbigsheep/Dreamstime: 5t, 27,28tc, 28tr, 28tcl,29cr, 29br. http://www.freepik.com Designed by Freepik: front cover b/g, 1. Werner Forman Archive: 15c, 16tr, Granger HPA/Alamy: 21cl. Hupeng/Dreamstime: 12t bg. The Image Works/Topfoto: 10l, 12tl, 12cl. Lorraine Logan/Shutterstock: 16b. Mikhail Nekrasov/ Dreamstime: 4 David Parker/Alamy: 2, 26, 28c, 28cr, 28bl, 28bc, 29tl, 29tr, 29cl, 29bl. PFH/BAL: front cover cl, 6c, 8br, 9t, Seasun/Shutterstock: 6-7 bg, 8-9 bg. CC Wikimedia Commons: front cover cr, 1c, 3, 5b,7c, 8bl, 11c, 12cr, 13cl, 13cr, 14c, 15 bg, 16tl, 17b, 18c, 19c, 20l, 20c, 21cl, 21cr, 22, 23, 24tl, 24c, 24r, 25cl, 25c, 25cr, 28tl, 28bcl, 28br, 29tc, 29c, 29bc.
Every attempt has been made to clear copyright. Should there be any inadvertent omission please apply to the publisher for rectification.

HB ISBN: 978 1 4451 5192 2
PB ISBN: 978 1 4451 5193 9

Printed in China

Franklin Watts
An imprint of
Hachette Children's Group
Part of The Watts Publishing Group
Carmelite House
50 Victoria Embankment
London EC4Y 0DZ

An Hachette UK Company
www.hachette.co.uk
www.franklinwatts.co.uk

Contents

Chinese mythology

The myths and legends of ancient China are some of the oldest in the world, dating back nearly 4,000 years. The myths come from many different cultural groups, and they include stories about how the world came to be, as well as folk tales and stories with a religious message. The stories are full of gods, monsters, animals, ghosts and nature spirits.

Myths and history

History and myth in ancient China were not always seen as separate. Some historical figures were worshipped as gods, and some of the stories were believed to be about events that really happened. Many of the myths changed and evolved over hundreds – or even thousands – of years of history, and there are several different versions of many stories.

Three religions

Some of the earliest myths deal with natural forces and beings such as rain, mountains, animals and the sun and moon. Then, more than 2,000 years ago, two new religious philosophies began: Taoism and Confucianism. Some myths were changed slightly and others were created to tie in with these new ways of thinking. When Buddhism arrived from India, some of its gods and stories were adopted by the Chinese.

After Buddhism arrived in China, beautiful temples were built. They are designed to inspire inner peace.

Gods in Chinese mythology

Many of the gods in Chinese mythology started as humans and were deified because of their great deeds. Other gods were part animal, such as Fuxi, who had a human head and a snake's body. Some of the gods in Chinese myths kept the universe running as it should.

The Jade Emperor was one of the most important gods. He ruled over the heavens in the same way that the human emperor down on Earth ruled China.

How do we know?

For many years, myths and stories in ancient China were passed down orally. Parents would tell them to their children, or people would listen to professional storytellers. Later, they started to be written down. Most of these writings have come down to us in bits and pieces, so it is sometimes hard to fit different versions of the same stories together.

Chinese myths feature some very fierce monsters!

Huangdi and Chiyou

Read their story on pages 8-9.

Fact file: Huangdi

Huangdi is often known as the Yellow Emperor. Legend says that he was born in about 2704 BCE, ruled for many years and became an immortal after he died. Most modern scholars think that he was a mythical character, not a real person.

Huangdi was a strong leader, but he also changed daily life for the people of China. According to the legends, he showed them how to build homes and grow crops, as well as inventing boats, the calendar, bows and arrows and many other things.

Huangdi in his own words:

Busy, busy, busy:
You should have seen this place before I got here, but I've done my best to improve it. I've come up with loads of new ideas, like maths and astronomy.

Coolest kit:
I have a war chariot with a statue on it that always points south. No matter what the conditions are, I know where I'm going.

Favourite colour:
What else could it be but yellow?

That's a lot of candles:
I lived to be over one hundred years old!

Fact file: Chiyou

Chiyou was a fierce warrior who was the leader of the Nine Li tribes. He was loved by his own people, but outsiders saw him as a frightening war god with a bull's head and sharp horns. Some stories say that he had four eyes and birds' feet.

Chiyou invented many different kinds of weapons, including the lance, arrow and shield. Armed with these weapons, his army was extremely strong. Led by Chiyou, they often attacked other tribes.

Chiyou in his own words:

Keeping it in the family:
I have 81 brothers, all as fierce as me. They can really take a punch – their foreheads are made of iron!

Party trick:
I can create really dense fog. It's great for confusing my enemies on the battlefield.

Fighting dirty:
My strength and weapons are usually enough to win a battle, but if not, I can call on ghosts and evil demons to join the fight.

Words to live by:
I'd rather die than lose a fight.

Clash of the gods

It looks like it's all about to kick off on the plains of Zhoulu. The forces of Huangdi are preparing for battle with Chiyou and his army. Our reporter will be live-blogging all the latest developments.

9:42 am – From where I'm standing I can see the fighters massing down on the plains. On one side, the army of the Yellow Emperor, and on the other side, Chiyou waits at the head of his own troops.

10:14 – And it's started! The first to rush into the fray are Chiyou's 81 brothers. Their iron foreheads glint in the sun as they race towards Huangdi's troops.

10:25 – Looks like Huangdi's not at all fazed by the attack of Chiyou's brothers. He has a group of gods with him - I think I can see the winged dragon Yinglong among them - and they're standing their ground.

11:10 – Nearly an hour in, and it looks fairly evenly matched. Chiyou's army are launching attack after attack, but Huangdi's army are beating them back.

Huangdi and Chiyou

CHARGE!

12:02 pm - A thick fog has descended on the battlefield, so it's hard to tell what's going on. Could this be Chiyou's doing? He can control the weather.

12:29 - I still can't see what's going on, but by the sound of it, Huangdi's army is taking a hammering. He needs to come up with a strategy to deal with this fog, or the battle will be over.

13:51 - Huangdi's army have just broken out of the fog! At the front is the emperor himself, driving his famous south-pointing chariot. It must have guided him out of the fog.

14:23 - For the last few minutes Huangdi's soldiers have been staggering around, looking dazed. It looks like Chiyou's lieutenant, Chimei, had confused them with black magic. But then one of Huangdi's men blew a cow horn - the loudest noise I've ever heard - and they all seem back to normal now.

15:07 - It's not looking good for Chiyou at the moment. Huangdi is beating a war drum; it's obvious that he smells victory.

15:43 - And that's that! Yinglong has captured Chiyou and brought him to Huangdi in chains. The great Battle of Zhoulu is at an end.

Hou Yi and Chang'e

Read their story on pages 12–13.

Fact file: Hou Yi

Hou Yi was a god with a talent for archery. He is famous for saving the day after the ten suns, which normally took turns travelling across the sky, all decided to rise at once. Having all ten suns shining made enough heat to shrivel the crops and cause a drought.

Hou Yi was asked to help, so he shot down nine of the suns. The spirit of each sun transformed into a three-legged raven and fell to Earth. He left the tenth, as the people still needed a sun. The suns' father was angry that Hou Yi had killed them, and banished him to live as a mortal.

Hou Yi in his own words:

Everybody loves me:
Well, everybody except for Di Jun, the father of the suns. He's not pleased that I shot down nine of them.

Home sweet home:
My wife and I have got a nice place now, but I really miss heaven. The views are so much better!

A slight misunderstanding:
Okay, so I ended the drought by shooting down the suns. But just because I helped the mortals doesn't mean that I want to be one!

Fact file: Chang'e

Chang'e was a goddess and the beloved wife of Hou Yi. When he was exiled from heaven to live as a mortal, she went with him. She found it difficult to adjust to her new life, and Hou Yi was often away, leaving her lonely.

Hou Yi was struggling, too, and he had an affair with a river goddess, leaving Chang'e even more isolated. Hou Yi was desperate to become immortal again, and he visited another goddess to ask for a pill that would make him immortal – but he didn't tell his wife.

Chang'e in her own words:

Love and marriage:
I love my husband, really I do. But I can't get rid of the feeling that he's hiding something from me.

If only I could:
Go back to the heavens to live with the other gods again. It's no fun down here on Earth.

Biggest weakness:
I'm a bit nosy. Tell me not to look at something, and I can't help myself!

Favourite animal:
I've always been fond of rabbits.

Gone girl

Rumours have been swirling ever since the lovely Chang'e disappeared from her home several weeks ago. Her husband, Hou Yi, is refusing to comment. So what really happened?

It's only been a few years since Hou Yi and Chang'e were exiled from the heavens. Hou Yi had angered Di Jun by shooting down his suns. But Chang'e had done nothing wrong, so it was a sign of her devotion to her husband that she followed him into exile as a mortal.

But now it seems that there was trouble brewing in paradise. "They started to grow apart," said one of the goddess's close friends. "Neither of them really liked living as mortals. I mean, would you? And then there were the rumours that Hou Yi was having an affair with that gorgeous river goddess, Luo Shen. Chang'e was heartbroken when she heard about that."

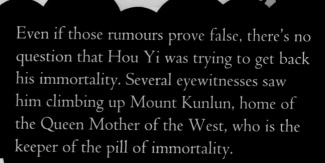

Even if those rumours prove false, there's no question that Hou Yi was trying to get back his immortality. Several eyewitnesses saw him climbing up Mount Kunlun, home of the Queen Mother of the West, who is the keeper of the pill of immortality.

"Hou Yi may have got the pill, but he certainly didn't take it himself," Chang'e's friend told us. "He's still here on Earth, isn't he?"

So if Hou Yi didn't take the pill, who did? Some people have speculated that perhaps he kept it at his home, waiting for the right moment. What if Chang'e, looking for a solution to her troubles, then found it?

The pill of immortality

A washerwoman who lives nearby believes this theory. On the night that Chang'e disappeared, she was walking past the goddess's house when she saw her through the window, putting something in her mouth.

Chang'e gasped and suddenly flew out of the window, her long, flowing robes billowing out behind her as she rose up into the sky.

"She was heading towards the moon," the washerwoman told us. "She was out of sight within minutes. But if you look carefully, even now, you can see a woman's figure on the moon. Poor girl, stuck up there on her own. Chang'e must have taken the pill, and now she's the goddess of the moon."

Da Yu and Nujiao

Read their story on pages 16–17.

Fact file: Da Yu

Da Yu (meaning 'Yu the Great') was one of ancient China's most popular heroes. Long ago, a great flood swept across the land for many years, driving people from their homes. Da Yu's father, Gun, tried to stop it, but he couldn't.

After Gun's death, Da Yu continued his work. He worked tirelessly for many years, sometimes so hard that he neglected his own family. Once he finally had the floods under control, he became emperor.

Da Yu in his own words:

Problem solving:
My father tried building dams to stop the floods, but I've been digging canals and irrigation channels instead. I think it will work better.

Helping hand:
When I need extra help, I call in my friends. One's a dragon and another's a tortoise – they never let me down.

Hobbies:
I don't have time for hobbies!

Greatest regret:
I would love to spend more time with my wife, but I'm sure she understands that duty comes first. (At least, I hope she does.)

Fact file: Nujiao

Nujiao was a beautiful young woman from the land of Tushan. When he met her, Da Yu was nearing the age of 30 – an age when most men were already married. He had seen an omen of a white fox with nine tails, which he believed meant that he would marry a girl from Tushan.

Although Nujiao loved her husband, she didn't see much of him. Da Yu spent most of their marriage away fighting the floods. One version of the story says that he was away for 13 years straight. During that time he passed his house three times but didn't come in.

Nujiao in her own words:

Doing my bit:
The sooner Da Yu gets those floods under control, the sooner he can come home. So I try to help, by making him packed lunches and such.

Keeping busy:
I hardly ever see my husband, so it gets a bit lonely. I keep busy with weaving, and tidying, and gardening … oh, who am I kidding? It's so boring, stuck here on my own!

Identity crisis:
In some versions of the story I'm called Tushan–shi and in others I'm Nujiao. It's so confusing!

15

A slight misunderstanding

Da Yu

Nujiao

I can't believe what's happened. My beautiful wife is gone, and it's all my fault!

I know I haven't always been the best husband – these floods have kept me too busy. But I would never do anything to hurt Nujiao.

The worst thing is that all she was doing was trying to help! I was in the middle of digging a tunnel through a mountain. It's hungry work, and Nujiao was great about bringing me snacks. We had a system: I would beat a drum whenever I needed food, and she would come. (Her cooking is amazing!)

Digging a tunnel through a mountain is not an easy job. I often transform into a bear when I'm working (it's one of my special skills) and it gives me extra strength, which makes the tunnelling go faster. But it's not very dignified, so I don't let Nujiao see me when I'm like that.

Grrrrr!

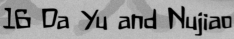

Yesterday I was working 'beary' hard (see what I did there?), and getting hungry, but I didn't want to call Nujiao. She's pregnant, you know, and nearly ready to give birth, so I wanted to give her a chance to rest.

But I must have stepped on the drum by mistake, because she came, carrying a basket of food. And when she arrived, she saw a massive bear, digging away at the earth with his long, sharp claws.

She was terrified. Can you blame her?

So she took off running, as fast as she could. I chased after her, trying to explain, but I forgot to change back into my human form first. I was only scaring her more.

Nujiao had reached the foot of the mountain when she turned back to look at me. She was so frightened that she began to turn into a stone! By the time I arrived, all that was left of my wife was a statue.

I cried out to the gods, asking for mercy. The belly of the statue split open, and there was my baby son. I'm going to raise him properly, I swear, and give him all the attention I was never able to give Nujiao.

Once I'm done sorting these floods, that is.

Aaaargh!

Gao Xin and Panhu

Read their story on pages 20-21.

Fact file: Gao Xin

Gao Xin was one of China's five legendary emperors. He is sometimes called Emperor Ku or the White Emperor. As a boy, he was known for being very clever, and he helped his father rule. After his father died, he took over as emperor.

According to legend, Gao Xin had at least four wives, and they all had sons who went on to do great things. Gao Xin also had at least two daughters, and finding a husband for one of them turned out to be more trouble than he had bargained for.

Gao Xin in his own words:

Awesome ancestors:
My great-grandfather was the famous Yellow Emperor. I try to live up to his legend!

Travelling in style:
In the autumn and winter, I ride a horse (like any normal emperor) but in spring and summer I switch to a dragon — much more impressive!

Favourite hobby:
I love music more than almost anything else. I've invented loads of musical instruments, and I've written some pretty great songs too.

Fact file: Panhu

Panhu was a dog, but not just any old mutt. One day, Gao Xin's wife had a terrible earache. A wizard came to see what he could do, and he pulled a strange golden cocoon out of her ear.

The queen kept the cocoon in a jar, covered with a plate. The cocoon soon hatched into a dog. She named him Panhu and kept him in the palace as a much-loved pet.

Panhu in his own words:

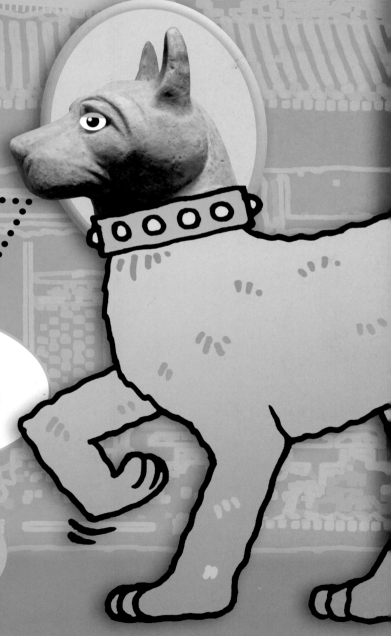

What's in a name?
I was named because of how I was born – *pan* means 'plate' and *hu* means 'jar'. I guess it's like a baby bird being named 'nest' or a bee being named 'hive'!

Where my loyalties lie:
The emperor and his wife have been good to me. I'd do anything to help them out.

Secret skills:
Whatever I set out to do, I get results. But sometimes it's best not to inquire too deeply into my methods, if you know what I mean …

狗 Man's best friend (Gao Xin's diary) 狗

THIRD DAY OF XINGYUE*:

Even though he rules a different kingdom, that idiot Fang causes me nothing but trouble! Just today I announced to all my courtiers that whoever brings me his head can marry my daughter. Maybe that will get results!

THE NEXT DAY:

The wife's been in a real state today – her dog's disappeared. I've sent servants to look for him.

Fang's head

FOUR DAYS LATER:

Panhu's finally come back home – carrying Fang's head with him! I don't know how he did it and, quite frankly, I don't care. I've told the palace kitchen to prepare their best roast and give it to the dog.

THREE DAYS LATER:

For three days we've been offering Panhu the best food we have, but he won't eat! He can't be annoyed that I didn't keep my promise about marrying my daughter, can he? I mean, he's a dog!

THE NEXT DAY:

Panhu still wouldn't eat today, so I gave him a pat on the head and asked what was bothering him. Imagine my amazement when he started to talk! He said he understood that I didn't want my daughter to marry a dog. (And what father would, I ask you?) But he said that if I covered him with a golden bell and left him for seven days, he would turn into a man. So even though it sounds crazy, I'm going to try it. He did get rid of my worst enemy, after all.

* The second month of the lunar calendar.

FIVE DAYS LATER:

Well, we're five days in, and I can't help wondering what's going on underneath that golden bell. But Panhu made me promise not to touch it until seven days had passed.

THE NEXT DAY:

Disaster! My wife was getting more and more worried about Panhu, because he hadn't had anything to eat or drink for days. And even though there was only one day left to go, she insisted on lifting up the bell to check on him. And there was Panhu – only he hadn't finished changing into a human yet! He has the body of a man, but the head of a dog. It's better than nothing, I guess, so I'd better prepare for the wedding …

Zhinu and Niulang

Read their story on pages 24–25.

Fact file: Zhinu

Zhinu was a beautiful young fairy who specialised in weaving. She lived in the heavens with her sisters and her parents, but she sometimes found it boring. One day she went down to Earth and met Niulang.

Once she was missed, her mother came down to Earth to find her and bring her back to the heavens. Zhinu was distraught at the idea of being separated from Niulang, but she was given no choice – she had to go back to her old life.

Zhinu in her own words:

Greatest skill:
I can weave anything. Amazingly soft silk, fluffy colourful clouds … you name it. I'm the queen of the loom!

Can't live without:
My beloved husband Niulang, or our son and daughter. We're a very happy little family.

Favourite animal:
I'm rather partial to magpies these days!

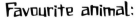

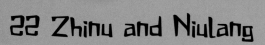

Fact file: Niulang

Niulang was a poor and humble cowherd. After his parents died, he lived with his older brother and his wife, but he didn't get on with his sister-in-law. Things got worse and worse, until Niulang had to leave and make his own way, with only a cow for company.

When he met Zhinu, it was love at first sight. She was bathing with her sisters in a lake, and Niulang hid her dress so that she wouldn't be able to go back to the heavens with her sisters. Once they were gone, he returned the dress, apologised, and asked her to marry him.

Niulang in his own words:

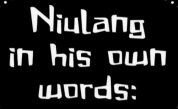

Favourite animal:
I love all cows — you have to, in my line of work! But the one I've had since childhood is a really good friend now.

I'd do anything for:
My beloved wife Zhinu. I was so lonely before I met her, but she's by far the best thing that ever happened to me!

Life is good:
We're poor, but we're happy. I look after the cows and the farm, she weaves the most amazing soft furnishings, and we both dote on our two children.

I'm late, I'm late!

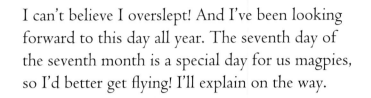

I can't believe I overslept! And I've been looking forward to this day all year. The seventh day of the seventh month is a special day for us magpies, so I'd better get flying! I'll explain on the way.

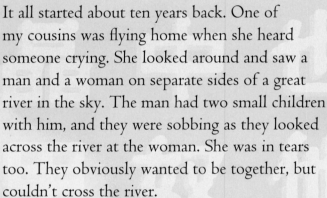

It all started about ten years back. One of my cousins was flying home when she heard someone crying. She looked around and saw a man and a woman on separate sides of a great river in the sky. The man had two small children with him, and they were sobbing as they looked across the river at the woman. She was in tears too. They obviously wanted to be together, but couldn't cross the river.

Speaking of my cousin, I can see her ahead with the other magpies. I'm miles behind them – I'd better speed up!

Anyway, my cousin was so upset by what she saw that she couldn't stop thinking about it. She knew how sad she'd be if she were ever separated from her chicks. So she asked around to find out what was going on.

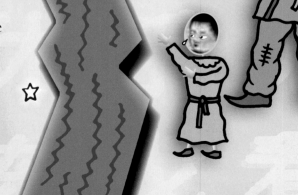

It turns out that the woman was Zhinu, daughter of the Jade Emperor. She had married a mortal, Niulang, and her parents were furious about it. So her mother arrived one day and dragged her back to the heavens, making her leave her husband and children behind. Can you imagine?

Anyway, Niulang's magical cow helped him follow them, but the goddess used her hairpin to scratch a river in the sky to separate him from his wife. The next day, they were all still there, sobbing their hearts out. So my cousin hatched a plan, and called in all the other magpies.

We arrived in our thousands, ready to help. There were so many of us that we almost filled the sky! Wing to wing, we packed together, until we formed a bridge across the river. Then Zhinu walked across to hug her husband and children. You should have seen their faces — they were so happy!

Since then, we've come back every year to form a bridge and give them one day together. I've never missed it, and I'm not going to miss this one. You'll have to excuse me — I've got work to do!

Monkey and the Jade Emperor

Read their story on pages 28–29.

Fact file: Monkey

Monkey's real name was Sun Wukong, but he is often just called 'Monkey', or sometimes 'the Monkey King'. He has a wide range of magical powers, which help him on his many fantastic adventures.

According to legend, Monkey was born from a stone. His magical powers and mischievous nature meant that he often caused trouble. Later in life, he went on a long journey to India and central Asia to help bring sacred Buddhist writings back to China.

Monkey in his own words:

Weapon of choice:
My magical staff weighs several tonnes and can grow or shrink on my command. When I'm not using it, I shrink it to the size of a needle and tuck it behind my ear.

Now you see me:
I can travel halfway around the world in a single somersault. Now that's fast!

Secret fear:
My powers mean that I don't have to be scared of much, but I have to admit that I don't like the idea of dying. Not one bit.

Fact file: The Jade Emperor

The Jade Emperor was one of the most important Chinese gods. From his home in the heavens, he was in charge of organising how all life ran. He goes by many names, including Yuhuang and Yu Ti.

The Jade Emperor was known for being wise and fair. In his early days he spent many years on Earth, trying to make life better for the mortals who lived there. One legend says that he chose the 12 animals that now make up the Chinese zodiac.

The Jade Emperor in his own words:

My ideal world:
A place for everything, and everything in its place. I've got no time for the kind of chaos that Monkey creates.

Best seat in the house:
From my heavenly throne, I can keep an eye on everything that goes on in the world below.

The host with the most:
Every few thousand years I invite a few select immortals to a banquet. I always serve the magical peaches that keep us immortal.

The peach thief

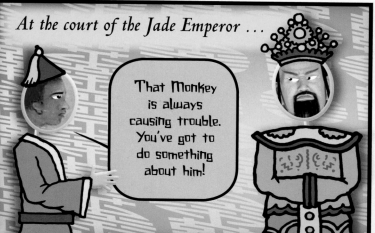

Glossary

ancestor a person from whom someone is descended, usually further back than a grandparent

archery the sport of using a bow to shoot arrows

Buddhism a religion or way of thinking that was started in India about 2,500 years ago. Buddhists focus on peace, kindness and wisdom

chariot a carriage with two wheels that is pulled by horses, often used in battle

Chinese zodiac a 12-year astrological cycle, where each year is ruled by the characteristics of one of 12 animals. In Chinese belief, if you were born in, say, the year of the rooster (2017), this will affect your personality

cocoon a case that protects the developing young of an insect

Confucianism a way of thinking based on the teachings of Confucius, who lived in China about 2,500 years ago

courtier person who is part of the household and entourage of a king or other ruler

cowherd a person whose job is looking after cattle

deified worshipped as a god

emperor ruler of a large area of land called an empire

exiled forced to leave your home and go and live somewhere else

folk tale a story that has its beginning in popular culture and is usually passed on by word of mouth

immortal living forever and never dying or decaying. Gods and goddesses are usually immortal

irrigation bringing water to fields of crops by digging channels for water to flow through

loom a machine used for making fabric by weaving thread

mortal an ordinary person who will eventually die instead of living forever

myth a traditional story that tries to explain why the world is the way that it is, or to recount legendary events

omen an event or sight that is believed to predict that something will happen

orally passed down by word of mouth from one person to another, rather than being written down

philosophy a particular way of thinking about the world and people's role in it

staff a long, straight stick that can be used as a weapon

Taoism a religion or way of thinking based on the teachings of Lao-tzu, which focuses on being virtuous and living in harmony with nature

universe all of time and space and its contents — everything that exists

Books

Ancient China (Explore!)
Izzi Howell, Wayland

Ancient China (DK Eyewitness Books),
Arthur Cotterell, Dorling Kindersley

Monkey King, Volume 1: Birth of the Stone Monkey,
Wei Dong Chen, JR Comics

Treasury of Chinese Folk Tales,
Shelly Fu and Patrick Yee, Tuttle Publishing

Websites

This website gives more information about religion in ancient China
http://quatr.us/china/religion/

Go here to find out more about life in ancient China:
www.dkfindout.com/us/history/ancient–china/

You'll find more information about Monkey and his adventures on this website:
www.britishcouncil.org/voices–magazine/monkey–king–worlds–most–popular–superhero

Use this website to learn more about Chinese mythology and search for individual gods:
www.godchecker.com/pantheon/chinese–mythology.php

Index

These are the lists of contents for each title in Stars of Mythology.

女　妻　太　明　西　信

子　木　立　白　上　我

好　李　小　旦　下　你

安　栖　少　晶　中　也

字　人　尖　甲　奴　他

家　大　田　早　友　目

家　天　力　休　手　见

象　夫　男　东　戈　看